Your Daddy Wasn't Shit, so You're Not Going to be Shit

YOUR DADDY WASN'T SH*T

SO YOU'RE NOT GOING TO BE SH*T

Removing the harmful effects of curse words

BY CARLOS MUHAMMAD

FOREWORD BY DAVID GLOVER
THE CONTROVERSIAL COUNSELOR

Printed in the United States of America: CreateSpace

Cover design, interior layout, and editing by WillowRaven Illustration & Design Plus.

ISBN-13: 978-0692696064 (Luv4self Publishing)
ISBN-10: 0692696067

LUV4SELF PUBLISHING

To my daughter Sanaa Fatirah Muhammad, never accept limitations. You are amazingly great and can be whatever you desire.

Table of Contents

Foreword

I am honored to have the opportunity to write the forward to **Your Daddy Wasn't Shit, so You're Not Going to be Shit**. This book is special to me because I am the biological brother of Carlos Muhammad. I am also the Author of the books *Cocktail Conversations* and *Real Talk-Real Conversations*. I know, this isn't about me, but when you read the following words you'll find out why this information is important.

The title of the book, **Your Daddy Wasn't Shit, so You're Not Going to be Shit**, is near and dear to me because I heard this kind of message all too many times. Although they were not the exact words my father used, his word choice was just as hurtful. I was told repeatedly how I was going to be soft and a "pussy." These words were expressed by my father whenever I wasn't performing athletically to his standards. His method of motivation, however, was not very motivational. As a result of his inability to choose the right words, the cycle my father started was passed down to me and I ultimately became very critical of Carlos and used similar words. The saying is true, hurt people hurt people. Carlos had absolutely no interest in sports, and because of his lack of interest in sports, I criticized him. As a child, Carlos continued to dance to the beat of his own drum and was clearly more interested in art related activities regardless to how much I hurt him. His passions were writing, reading comic books and drawing pictures with urban images. He was also constantly writing rap lyrics or using his wild imagination when playing with his toys.

Carlos was always multi-talented and skilled in his crafts; the problem is he didn't understand how talented he was, even though he would always excel. This book, ***Your Daddy Wasn't Shit, so You're Not Going to be Shit***, is coming during a perfect time when many young men and women hear negative messages on a daily basis. The impact of what they hear ultimately leaves a lasting impact and stunts their growth to succeed. In this book, there are many lessons to be learned. Over the years, I had to learn to encourage others to pursue their specific talents. All of our passions may be different but we must learn to appreciate others for what they are great at doing and using the right words. I now realize, unlike my father, that everyone will not make it in a sports related career; in fact, that number is slim to none.

I've also learned that in life things come around two-fold. Carlos was an inspiration for me to become an Author and when I began working on my second book it actually inspired him to dust off his cobwebs of creativity and come back hard as hell. Carlos is an amazing talent and every time he delivers a product you will see his talents unfold. In my opinion, he is the total package; Artist, Writer, Author, Lyricist, and Poet. After reading this book the only thing you will be able to say, like me is "damn isn't Carlos the Shit?"

The Controversial Counselor
David Glover

Preface

Ok, by now you're probably wondering, why would someone name a book a title such as this? This is disturbing, this is insane. This man has gone mad and clearly has no intention of selling this book. Truthfully, I didn't write this book to sound like what is traditionally accepted in the literary world. I wrote this book to speak in terms that you understand them and in a way that you understand. This book will resonate with some while turning off others before they actually get past the title and read it. So be it.

Let's be honest for a minute, the world we live in is harsh, cruel and as insane as this book sounds. The womb becomes a cemetery for a fetus even before making its grand entrance. Upon conception, the vultures prey on babies and nurture them until they become a part of some classification. This is where we get the have, have-nots, the producers, consumers and the rich, middle class and poor.

Sadly, some of us grow up in homes that unknowingly contribute to negative societal trends. The daily routine, verbal and nonverbal communication that our families are engaged in is sometimes so toxic that we literally develop as waste product. Unfortunately, many settle because being waste product is the highest compliment, and becoming less than that, is the greatest offense. Mean spirited people come along and continue to remind us that we're not SHIT. That is a major problem in a world where the aim in life is to be the shit and when you're not shit nobody will give a shit about you.

Now, isn't that some shit?

Ok, Carlos enough with the foul language. How can someone that serves as an educator and stand before our young people use such language? This language is highly offensive and repulsive. I wouldn't debate that. Although this language may be rightfully criticized, some of our wrongfully used language without pro-fane words is actually more problematic. Furthermore, if these words caught your attention I did my job.

Prologue

A wise man once said, "Set yourself in Heaven NOW". He went on to advise that we "secure ourselves some benefits while living which are *luxury, money, good homes and friendships in all walks of life*". These tangible things nobody can deny will provide a greater sense of comfort and tranquility. If you don't have them, why not? Are you *really* living? If not, why not? What is life to you? Do you believe you're living simply because you're breathing or are you really just in animated dead person?

What happens with the choices we make, since everything we are taught is a choice? What about our thoughts? Are we asking ourselves will I succeed or will I fail? Will I become trapped or live freely? Will I "try" to do something or make it happen? Will I become rich or live poor? Everyone has a journey. In truth, we all start out the same but our ending is a result of our thinking that lead to the choices we make. Often we allow the misuse and abuse of words from others to determine our fate. We have heard many people say no one can predict their "faith" but the truth is someone can.

Words can be powerful, uplifting or destructive in determining your path. How you internalize, receive, perceive and believe them is what actually matters. Ultimately what you *think* or *accept* is what you will become. You can, however, make a choice to control what you embrace or reject. You can make a choice to decide the path that you will take. You can control what you *think* and determine your fate. These are choices you can make. Hopefully, this book will help you to look at what you have personally accepted so you can make those changes. Hopefully, you will decide to remove the *curse words* you have accepted and set yourself in heaven NOW.

Dedrick Muhammad
Co-Founder and CFO of Luv4self Enterprises

In the beginning was the Word...

Two babies were born on May 25, 1972. They both lived in the same neighborhood. One baby (**Baby B**) became a vagrant, his daily duties consisted of waking up on his curbside and walking to the intersection with a cardboard sign saying "feed me, I'm hungry" and the other baby (**Baby A**) became a millionaire. The millionaire's daily routine consisted of waking up in some remote vacation spot checking his earnings. Both babies were born in the same hospital. Both babies grew up, went to school, ate, used the bathroom, puked, farted and observed the crazy world around them.

What happened that took these two babies on two totally different paths as adults?

TURN THIS PAGE AND FIND OUT...

Fuck you...

> **Bitch...**

> > **Piece of Shit...**

> > > **Mother Fucker...**

> > > > **Asshole...**

> > > > > **Pussy...**

Whew,! Now that I got that off my chest, just insert your favorite obscene, profane and repulsive expletives that are commonly referred to as "curse words" and none of them can come remotely close to telling someone that they "*can't*" achieve something or they will "*never*" be able to accomplish something.

Telling someone to "fuck off" probably has less of a damaging effect on someone's psyche than telling them some word that places psychological limitations on them. I have elected to refer to these crippling words as **"curse words"**.

Curse Words

How "Curse" has been traditionally defined

A curse in the traditional sense has been an expression used to explain a "spell" that has been cast on someone that would prohibit them from doing something.

Think about that.

Webster defines it as:

1: *a prayer or invocation for harm or injury to come upon one:* <u>*IMPRECATION*</u>
2: *something that is* <u>*CURSED*</u> *or accursed*
3: *evil or misfortune that comes as if in response to imprecation or as retribution*
4: *a cause of great harm or misfortune:* <u>*TORMENT*</u>
5: <u>*MENSTRUATION*</u> *—used with the*

The most common usage of the word, however is always in reference to the profane or vulgar. Webster refers to these as transitive verbs and has defined them as:

1: *profanely insolent language against* <u>*BLASPHEME*</u> *<curse God and die — Job 2:9*
2a: *to call upon divine or supernatural power to send injury upon <was cursed and fears he will die>*
    b: *to execrate in fervent and often profane terms <cursed by future generations unless we act now>*
3: *to bring great evil upon* <u>*AFFLICT*</u> *<a land cursed with famine>*

What I find interesting is that in any way in which the word is used, whether someone is being cursed/accursed or being cursed at, there is some form of condemnation. While one refers to someone evoking something "supernatural" and placing it on another person causing some state of stagnation, the latter also is used to "damn" someone. Neither is positive.

How negative thoughts/words can influence our behavior

I read some great books in college on cognitive behavior and how therapist in this field felt there was a relationship between thoughts, feelings and behaviors. If this is the case, how someone thinks and feels about themselves will determine how they act. Think for a second about every person you consider a *low life, a loser, a waste of sperm* or an *abortion that lived.* No seriously, take a few minutes to think about the person you think the least of, even if it's you and almost undoubtedly at the root of that person's behavior is a negative thought about themselves. Interestingly, these people don't just come out of a vacuum. They emerge as a result of thoughts, emotions, words and an environment that perpetuates what they have grown to accept.

Additionally, it is not always what has been said continuously to them, but how they *receive, perceive and believe* what was being said and often *who says it* that mattered. **The human brain naturally picks up signals with each message it receives daily.** Each signal that is received and later perceived contains conceptual or emotional content. So, if the person conveying the message is *insignificant* their message may not contain *any information* for our brains to store, therefore, creating no perception. On the flip side, if the person is *significant* and you lay hold to their every word, it's a done deal. There is no mind over matter, everything they say matters. Unfortunately, because of the place they hold in our lives they have the ability to produce more of an arousal. Their words, tone of voice, context and most importantly intangibles like body language will matter more to us.

W. Clement Stone, the famous business man, self-help thinker and philanthropist has been popular for saying:

"You are a product of your environment. So choose the environment that will best develop you toward your objective. Analyze your life in terms of its environment. Are the things around you helping you toward success - or are they holding you back?"

What hasn't been said however is *what environment?* The environment we physically live in is less of a threat than the mental environment we developed over time and carry with us every day. So the things *around* us have less of an effect than the things we have *within us* (our thoughts). Remember, **Baby B** and **Baby A** both grew up in the same neighborhood, around similar circumstances but took on two totally different paths? One became a creator, in complete control of his destiny, while the other became a *good for nothing* victim.

"Curse Words" Redefined

While teaching Freshmen Seminar Classes on college campuses, I would do an exercise with my students. Whenever the topic of **"personal responsibility"** came up we would explore the differences in *victim* and *creator* language as explained by *Skip Downing* in his *On Course* textbook. I would first ask my students to explain the differences and an interesting dialog would always ensue.

The victim they learned is the person that always makes excuses and never takes personal responsibility for their failures. This person generally is a complainer, a blamer; they see their problems as permanent and focus on their weaknesses. The Creator on the other hand always accepts responsibility. This person is solution oriented; they turn complaints into requests and see problems as temporary. Creators are also doers and always striving to be better than their previous self. When I would ask the students how they see themselves, very seldom would someone say they are victims but a combination of both. Some of the more confident students would say they were creators emphatically.

I would then ask them what separated the Vagrant from the Millionaire since these were two extremes in the *best* and *worst* case scenarios on how humans can turn out *financially*. Both had choices, both came through the womb of a woman and went through the vicissitudes of life. There was however undeniably something that separated the two? One accepted the *curse words* they were told and the other one did not. Because I always believed everything has a root/origin and every problem has a root cause, I would take this conversation a step further. I would introduce the topic of *curse words* by asking the students to provide me with a list and I'll write them on the board.

"Go ahead, yell out some curse words" I'd say and the students would yell back:

BITCH
MOTHERFUCKER
ASSHOLE
PUSSY
SHIT
FUCK…

WHOA…I would abruptly stop them after about five of these obscene expletives and also before another colleague or high administrator walked pass my classroom wondering what kind of circus act I was pulling. I would then say to them "NO, listen to what I am asking you and answer again". Repeating myself I'd say slowly "Yell out some CURSE words"

There was always one that would yell out very confidently words like:

I'll try
I can't
I'll never be
I'm a failure
It's impossible

After emphasizing the word *curse* and the students taking their traditional understanding of the word and applying it to the context of the discussion they too understood the crippling and harmful effects of negative words that were accepted and *believed*. After having this discussion, we would generally agree that the victim seemingly was made a victim from the words they accepted and was not self-made. This is when we'd go into the *victimization of the victim*.

This topic would go something like this:

The victimization of the victim

People are generally very critical of people that exhibit what has come to be known as "victim" behavior". I'm sure most of us came across someone that is always making excuses, has a reason why they won't be able to do something or why they failed at something. Most of these people are also known for playing what is called the *blame game*. What most of us fail to do however is go to the root of why or how they came to think the way they do. What is the root cause?

We've all heard the expression; human beings are creatures of habit. What we have been saying essentially is that we process, learn and function by repeating something over and over again. This is not rocket science and you don't need someone to explain what you experience every day by going on a long drawn out tirade. Or do you? If repetition is the mother of *all* learning it's safe to assume we do have to hear things over and over again to get it. GET IT? So things have a tendency to stick with us and ultimately *become a part of us* when they are repeated.

Can you imagine being a child and repeatedly hearing negative messages over and over again? Of course, most of us can. What if an overwhelming amount of negative messages are repeated prior to conception? What if we were literally bombarded with negative messages on the second, on the minute, on the hour, on the day, in the months prior to conception? How might that impact us? Let's go back into the womb before the birth of a baby. Several studies indicate that the emotional and mental state of a mother while conceiving is very impactful on a child's psychological development.

In an article in **Emax Health** dated November 11, 2014, Kathleen Blachard wrote:

"Findings from researchers show a fetus receives chemical signals from mom during pregnancy that could have a negative impact on how a baby develops after birth. The psychological state of a mother – during pregnancy and after delivery - has a direct impact on the health of a baby after birth.

Curt A. Sandman, Elysia P. Davis, and Laura M. Glynn of the University of California-Irvine studied how a woman's psychological state during pregnancy and then after, affects the emotional state of babies, even before they're born.

Researchers know a variety of factors in the womb can affect a baby's health; some of which include smoking, alcohol intake and environmental exposure to toxins.

In their studies, researchers found babies can be depressed after they're born if mom is depressed during pregnancy and stayed depressed after giving birth."

Now let's put that in the context of what was previously mentioned. Can you imagine what a mother is passing on prior to conception when she is filled with doubt, insecurities and count-less negative thoughts like *curse words?* This fetus is literally in a toxic bag of water/amniotic sac. Sadly, every negative thought the mother is carrying creates a chemical reaction that alters her amniotic fluid. *Poor baby.*

To look at this from another angle, an amazing study was con-ducted by a man named Dr. Masaru Emoto who did research on water crystals and how negative words and energy can actu-ally alter the molecular structure of water. When negative words were spoken it literally changed the configuration of water crys-tals. How is this connected you ask? Since humans are about 70-75% water, his question was, how does this finding impact us? In looking for answers, He would conduct several experiments, playing certain kinds of music or uttering certain words to a bottle of water. He would then freeze it to see how the crystals would form.

He wrote:

"But our experimenting didn't stop there. We next thought about what would happen if we wrote words or phrases like "Thank you" and "Fool" on pieces of paper and wrapped that paper around the bottles of water with the words facing in. It didn't seem logical for water to "read" the writing, understand the meaning, and change its form accordingly. But I knew from the experiment with music that strange things could happen.

The results of the experiments didn't disappoint us. Water exposed to "Thank you" formed beautiful hexagonal crystals but water exposed to the word "Fool" produced crystals similar to the water exposed to heavy-metal music, malformed and fragmented."

---Dr. Masaru Emoto, Author of Hidden Messages in Water

Although several critics would later refer to Dr. Emoto's re-search and studies as pseudoscience, could it possibly have some validity in explaining the mental state that contributes to human development prior to conception? What effect would these negative words have on the amniotic sac/fluid of a pregnant woman carrying a fetus? What would they ultimately do to the fetus itself? What impact would these words have on adults' molecular structure since we are 70-75% water? Some students, of course, would still rush to debate these points and I'd have to reiterate my lesson about *repeated negative messages* by stating that:

Repetition is the mother of learning

I'd say something like this:

Ok, by now you're probably thinking I'm a wacko. That's fine. *Sticks and stones may break my bones but names will never hurt me* (smile). Furthermore, I believe that even with some emotional and psychological harm prior to conception, all is not lost. A child still comes into this world with the ability to escape a negative life. At the point of conception, they are only like a barely used USB (smile). The newborn now begins to learn by observing, copying and repeating what they see and hear around them. This information is then stored and more information is collected even if it is not accessed until needed.

We all know that taking one step never made any child walk but *repeatedly* taking steps *over and over* again does. Interestingly, repetition is literally the process in which humans master or become proficient at anything. *Yes, in order to become a great anything you have to continue to repeat everything.* It is just the way we are hard wired and it is no different with collecting information that gives us our self-esteem, world view or personal outlook on life. EVERYTHING IS LEARNED THROUGH REPETITION, EVEN NEGATIVE AND POSITIVE MESSAGES. So naturally if everyone significant in your life continued to state and reinforce limitations or curse words and you *believe them* you'll ultimately live a life of limitations. On the flip side if everyone

around did the exact opposite and you believed them you'll ultimately live a life free of limitations.

Just for clarity, I'm not saying Human Beings are these weak,
fragile creatures that we have to walk on eggshells with? No,
not exactly, but I am saying babies and children are these impressionable, fragile creatures that you have to walk lightly with
(smile). By the time they become adults, so much harm may be
done that they have to be reprogrammed. *A "Victim" mentality,
therefore, is the result of repetitious negative messages.* It's true; no
child enters the world making excuses, although they may be
filled with negative thoughts about themselves. If a child is not
bombarded with thoughts of what they can't do or will never
be capable of achieving, they can get past those feelings. Babies
and children naturally want to explore, express themselves and
conquer new daily tasks as they unfold. People around that child
foster and further develop a mentality and help to create what
the young child grows to perceive as their reality.

After this conversation with my students they'd continue asking questions, debate, disagree or agree in silence. This is when
I'd offer them extra credit to come to an event where I'd share a
short story about **Baby B** and **Baby A**.

You cursed me out
The Stage (Poetic interlude)

I am created by what others stated
About me
Defined me
Designed me with a combination
Of negative thoughts
Resulting in negative situations
Horrible affirmations
I am the mind
Of curse words intertwined
Rewiiiind...
I am not myself
My life was developed
Negative attitude enveloped
Packaged in my body
Delivered to the world
That released
constant
continuous
Curse words
Disbursed words
Nonstop,
refused to let up
My life was set up
Without my consent
I am not my own person
So in time, my personality worsened...

Let's take a look at **Baby B.**

Baby B had three siblings and a single mother that had a job that paid her barely enough money to feed her latchkey kids. Their dinner consisted primarily of chopped up boiled hot dogs mixed with pork and beans. On a good day, they ate Buffalo wings without any sauce or seasonings.

Yum, now isn't that highly nutritious?

Peanut Butter and Jelly was also on high rotation in their rat infested home. Often they'd sift through the rat pellet infested bread to find the good pieces before making a sandwich. Their father left when **Baby B** was about seven years old to pursue a life of loose women and drug addiction. Because **Baby B** and his younger sibling would constantly find themselves in trouble their mother would remind them that **"you're daddy wasn't shit so you're not going to be shit".**

In addition to their mothers beautifully and highly motivating words were the messages they conveyed to one another. Besides the normal daily abusive words like "you're ugly" you're a "sorry loser" (when they played the dozens) were the subtle but power-ful *curse words*. Some of those words included "you *can't*, you'll *never* be, you're not good enough, you're *not* smart enough" and "you've *always* been a failure". Yes, **Baby B** grew up in an environment where *cursing one another out* was the order of the day.

Generational Curse of Poverty

The words "***your daddy wasn't shit so you're not going to be shit***" is probably one of the most positive self-image messages a parent can give to a child. The power in those words are very uplifting, motivational and would encourage any young person to be better than, perhaps their "***wasn't shit dad***". If you have children consider doing this to encourage them.

WHY NOT?

Ok, I'm kidding.

In truth those words to a child can be a *huge inheritance* if his/her mental environment has nothing to counter those messages. It is like mentally and emotionally passing down failure and poverty.

Passing poverty down from generation to generation is a *mentality* that is never a good thing. Hell, who wants that kind of inheritance? POVERTY IS A STATE OF MIND. **Baby B**, however, cashed in on his inheritance or should I say cashed out? Yes, he cashed out for certain. Growing up with a *failures state of mind* would have him *out of cash* which ultimately made him *broke*. Broke bank account, broke wallet because of a broken spirit. We all know that *broke* things are in need of fixing. In religious circles they like to refer to the kind of inheritance **Baby B** received as the Generational Curse of Poverty. Economists like to refer to it as the Cycle of Poverty and believe that this cycle or *curse* occurs when resources are limited and there is little to no *intellectual*, social, cultural or financial capital. They also believe racism, broken families and other "negatives" can contribute greatly to this cycle. What economists fail to focus on is how *state of mind* is the major factor in creating this cycle as well as breaking it.

Don't curse at me

The Stage (Poetic interlude II)

Don't attempt to curse me with your words
Curse words
the worst words
uttered
never stammering or stuttered
No pause
Aimed directly with the aim to affect me
what's your cause?
No vulgarity exceeds the disparity
Between the regularity of unwanted charity
In the form of words
That breakdown forms
Watching a break down form
Not catching a break,
Down,
Sadly formed
from words
"TRY is to fail"
You "Can't" win
Can't you tell
You'll "NEVER" break from this spell
You're too "weak" to rebel
From curse words
The worst words
Non-positive selected adverse words
Uttered
and I refuse to believe them
because I don't need them.

Now let's take a look at **Baby A**.

Baby A also had three siblings and a single mother that had a job that paid her barely enough money to feed her children. **Baby A's** mother however received post-secondary education, receiving her Associates degree from a local community college. **Baby A's** mother worked as a teacher's assistant at one of the elementary schools, so this allowed her the time to make it home in order to prepare some sort of meal for her children. Their dinner consisted primarily of canned veggies, fried chicken, hamburgers and hotdogs and on a good day a huge baking pan of Macaroni and Cheese. Her children also ate lots of fruits and veggies for snacks. Her meal wasn't always the healthiest but her meals were prepared *out of love*.

In addition, **Baby A** and his siblings were required to attend church services on some weeknights, Bible Study and regular service on Sunday. Their father and mother unfortunately separated when **Baby A** was seven but they mutually decided to co-parent. Well, at least that's what they called it, considering that their father moved out of town, remarried and would see the children on holidays and summers. He did manage to pay his child support consistently and made sure the children didn't go without anything. He also had an Associate's Degree from the same college he met their mother years prior.

He was able to land a decent job out of town and would reinforce to his children the same thing their mother taught them that they *"can be and do anything"*. Both parents also told their children not to pick on other children and, more importantly, one another. Because **Baby A** grew up in the same neighborhood as Baby B they would often meet up along with other children in the neighborhood. Of course, Baby B and many of the other children that grew up similarly were used to name calling, playing the dozens and using vulgar language with one another. They thought **Baby A** was corny because he'd always tell them not to call him or anyone else names. They found it hilarious when he would yell "don't curse at me".

You are what you think about yourself

Baby B and **Baby A** both attended the same elementary school early on until Baby B was shipped off to an alternative school in the boondocks where there were no stores, no human life or civilization to prompt him to act out. If he decided to skip school he would be hanging out with Bambi, Chip and Dale or possibly Winnie the Pooh (smile).

Because **Baby B** was placed in Special Ed classes, he was on an I.E.P (Individualized Education Program) received Vyvanse pills and took high dosages of Methylphenidate (Ritalin) because of his behavioral problems. The teachers would often tell the children that were acting out that they would *never be anything of importance* with their behavior. They'd also tell them in an attempt to *motivate them* to do better that they *can't be doctors and lawyers* or a celebrity if they didn't do right. On *good days,* however, they would give incentives for good behavior.

Baby A was in classes with all the dorky, nerdy, *high achievers* and was always told in his classes how amazing he was. They'd always receive awards for the good grades they continued to receive. They'd attend conferences, go on college tours and were encouraged to apply for scholarships. **Baby B** and **Baby A** both stayed in those kinds of environments throughout middle school and high school. **Baby B** however only went to the 10th grade but he did return to get his G.E.D.

****

Back in the neighborhood was a different story. The *bad guys* were rewarded and the *good guys* were often teased and picked on. **Baby B** excelled and became more popular in this setting and his negative behavior made him cool among his peers. **Baby A** was viewed as a smart *cornball*. **Baby A** was often approached when he'd walk past the corner store where **Baby B** and some of the other kids in the neighborhood were hanging out. They'd ask **Baby A** to participate in some of their drinking and other self-destructive experimentations. They wanted him to share in their drugs of choice. **Baby A** however, was strong-willed, focused and would tell them without hesitation that he was "*good*" and didn't need a false high to make him feel better about himself. He sometimes would stand around and talk with them and state that he was *high on life*. His intentions were always to encourage them to do better.

Of course, sometimes this would make them feel he thought he was better than them, and that he was a goody two shoes, as opposed to a goody with one shoe (smile). The truth was they were projecting how they felt about themselves on him. They actually felt he was *better* and many of them secretly *wished* they had his will and determination to succeed. What they didn't realize however is that their behavior was a direct reflection of how they saw themselves. Because they had a low estimation of who they were, they did destructive things to themselves in the name of having fun. Because they didn't value the life they were living, they subconsciously and unconsciously did things that could potentially harm the very continuance of that life. They didn't see that because they thought nothing of themselves they were literally becoming nothing.

Fast Forward

As years progressed **Baby B** would make so many negative decisions that placed him in more horrible situations that he looked at his own life and wondered where he went wrong. Everything he *tried* failed. He was untalented, uneducated and felt he *couldn't do anything* right. He was bombarded with bills that he couldn't pay and ended up losing several low paying jobs and ultimately was evicted from the little studio apartment that he couldn't afford. *He wasn't shit because his daddy wasn't shit* seemed like self-fulfilling prophecy. **Baby B** ultimately ended up homeless, broke and depressed and his life was a living hell.

Baby A on the other hand seemed to make all the right decisions that placed him in predicaments to meet all the right people. He graduated with his Bachelors and Master's degree in business and ended up making investments, purchasing stocks, bonds, CD's, countless real estate and owned several successful businesses. All his investments paid off. He had millions of dollars and it seemed like his future was going to get even brighter. Occasionally, he'd take a ride in his old neighborhood to see where he came from and how far his life progressed.

****

One day while driving in his old neighborhood a man ran up to his car with a sign saying "feed me, I'm hungry". **Baby A** looked intensely at the man because his dirt filled face looked familiar. He rolled up his windows and locked his doors and continued driving. While driving **Baby A** couldn't stop thinking why that vagrant looked so familiar and how did this man allow his life to become such a mess that he ended up in this predicament. Then it dawned on him, that man was **Baby B**.

"Wow," he thought.

"We were born in the same hospital. Grew up in the same neighborhood, went to school, ate, used the bathroom, puked, farted and observed the crazy world around us, yet I am here and he's there".

He made an immediate U-turn and went back to talk to **Baby B** with intentions to give him some money. When **Baby B** approached the car and saw who it was **Baby A** and **Baby B** embraced with a friendly hug. **Baby A** told him to get in. The stench of sanitation permeated the car from **Baby B's** unwashed clothes that were more than likely worn as he went through trashcans and dumpsters looking for food.

Baby A reluctantly asked him, "What happened?"

Baby B responded, "Life happened."

His breath seeped into **Baby A's** nostrils.

Baby A retorted "It looks and smells like death happened, to me."

Baby B continued, "My mother repeatedly said to me, '***Your Daddy Wasn't Shit, so You're not Going to be Shit.***'"

"In life, most of us would narrow down the direction people take to *choices*. Although that is partly true, choices are *never* absent of how someone thinks. Everything starts from a thought. So your thoughts are like the motor for your choices. Sadly, the more negative people think the worse choices they will make. "**Your Daddy Wasn't Shit, so You're not Going to be Shit**" was not the nail in the coffin, but those words were reflective of the attitude that preceded the *curse words* I'd continuously hear. If I discussed something I wanted to pursue, I was told *I couldn't* do it followed by a million reasons why it wasn't possible. If I talked about somewhere I wanted to go I was told I *can't* afford this or I *can't* afford that instead of being encouraged to work on ways to make it happen. If I said I wanted to be something great in life I was told what I could *never* be because it would be difficult and nobody in our neighborhood did it and what made it worse is I believed those things instead of believing in me. **Baby A** although we lived in the same neighborhood our environment was different."

Baby A interjected, "You're making *poor* excuses for your failures and as they say, excuses are for the incompetent. If you can articulate all of these things you have the ability to change your situation."

Baby B responded, "You would think, right? Unfortunately, it's not that easy. If you've grown to believe you were limited in your abilities and what you were capable of achieving since child-hood, how likely are you to achieve anything of greatness? It's ultimately about what you believe and how much you *believe in yourself* that matters. I read a book once called the **Power of your Subconscious Mind** by a guy named Dr. Joseph Murphy that said, '*The law of life is the law of belief*'. My life is a clear reflec-tion of my beliefs and these beliefs were taught to me similarly to how a child is taught to believe whatever religion they were reared on since birth or in Santa, the Easter Bunny or the Tooth Fairy. As young impressionable children we're not developed enough to question things said to us because of who is saying them to us. So these beliefs become a part of us."

Baby A retorted, "Well you're an adult now, change your beliefs. To me it still sounds like you're *playing the victim and making a bunch of excuses.*"

Baby B chuckled and continued, "Have you ever influenced someone to change their religion?"

Baby A responded, "Why would I want to? People are free to believe what they want to believe."

Baby B asked, "Do you really believe that?"

Baby A shot back, "Yes, why wouldn't I?"

Baby B asked, "So why do parents teach children to believe what they believe which was likely taught to them from their parents and passed down for generations if people are really free to be-lieve what they want to believe?"

Baby A started to get equally frustrated with the conversation as well as the different smelly scents reeking from **Baby B's**

clothing and dry putrid breath, he then responded "what's your point and what does any of this have to do with what you've become in your life?

Baby B looked at him smiling, flashing his brownish yellow stain colored teeth with several missing; he then explained "It all starts at home. You are taught your foundations of belief as a child. If you're not taught early on to believe in *your own abilities* and there's no intervention in your educational environment, where do you stand? Instead of teaching children to *believe in limitations*, bombarding them with *curse words* and making things outside of them all powerful and almighty why aren't children taught to believe simply in their abilities and taught that they are capable of any and everything their minds can conceive? See, your parents may not have had it all but they had enough to give you *belief in yourself* that you felt capable of accomplishing what you have accomplished. My parents gave me enough *curse* words to make the choices I've made".

Baby A cut him off angrily and argued "wait, so you're going to blame this mess on your parents? Your mother worked hard to make sure you had food, clothing, shelter and a roof over your head and this is your display of gratitude? I was coming to help you but you're in worse shape than I imagined and you smell God awful. Please leave my car right now and maybe I'll check on you in a few days to see if you possibly got any sense in your head. What a disappointment you are to blame everyone around you instead of looking at yourself and realizing that you have the power to change your condition overnight if you just believe in yourself".

Baby B started exiting **Baby A's** car and looked at him smiling, flashing his brownish yellow stain colored teeth with several missing; he then ended "now you understand, I knew you would".

****

Days went by and **Baby A** couldn't help but to ponder on the strange conversation he had with **Baby B**. Interestingly, while sitting in his office he stumbled on a book he read called *Words Can Change Your Brain* by an Author named Dr. Andrew Newberg. In the book Dr. Newberg said:

"Without language, we find ourselves living in a state of emotional chaos. Our brain has given us the potential to communicate in extraordinary ways and the way we choose to do so can improve the neural functioning of the brain. In fact, a single word has the power to influence the expression of genes that regulate physical and emotional stress. If we do not continually exercise the brain's language centers, we cripple our neurological ability to deal with the problems we encounter with each other."

He then looked at some notes he wrote from a motivational Speaker and Author named Anthony "Tony" Robbins that said:

"Most of us don't realize, however, that the words you habitually choose also affect what you experience. Transformational Vocabulary is about **how you can take control of your habitual vocabulary to change the quality of your life.** *Simply by changing your habitual vocabulary—the words you consistently use to describe the emotions of your life—you can instantly change how you think, feel and how you live."*

After reading these words, **Baby A** was more puzzled because some of what both authors were saying resembled some of the things **Baby B** understood, articulated but *couldn't* find the power to live. **Baby A**, however, was now more intrigued to talk to **Baby B** and share some of what he read. He figured if **Baby B** could focus on changing his own vocabulary and replacing words that placed limitations and restrictions in his mind with words or phrases like *I can, I will,* I'm able, I'm capable, It's possible then he can start to look within for his source of power.

Taking BackWORDS forward

Baby A drove around the old neighborhood for days and strangely couldn't locate **Baby B**. He couldn't help to wonder if he somehow offended **Baby B** to the point of driving him over the edge. He became really concerned. Six weeks passed and **Baby A** decided to get out of his car and start asking around. Strangely nobody saw or could locate **Baby B**, he was lost. On week seven while **Baby A** was driving around in the neighborhood he had an impulse to drive in an alley. There he saw a naked man lying in a fetal position on the pavement between two trash cans.

"**Baby B,**" he yelled out.

Baby B lifted his head and stood up in a drunken stupor fully exposed. He smiled; flashing his brownish-yellow stain colored teeth with several missing and responded.

"Is that you **Baby A**? How did you find me?"

"I didn't" **Baby A** responded "my spirit directed me here."

Baby B walked towards him to give him a hug and **Baby A** stopped him in his tracks.

"NO SIR, not until you're fully clothed"

He then walked to his trunk and grabbed some clothes that he just picked up earlier from the cleaners and gave them to **Baby B** to put on. They fit perfectly. He then hugged him and told him that he wanted him to take a ride with him somewhere. **Baby B** having absolutely, positively nothing to do with his time didn't hesitate to take the ride and free heat (smile). They rode to a bookstore where a book signing was taking place and went in.

As they walked into the building words like *you can, you can do it, nothing is impossible, you will succeed* were placed in artistically designed frames on the wall. **Baby B** smiled flashing his brownish yellow stain colored teeth with several missing at **Baby A**. The ambiance in the room seemed to spiritually *connect* the two. This event they would learn would be their *defining moment.* In some strange way, this place seemed to give both of their lives *meaning.* While taking a seat, they took in more of the energy from the dark, smoke-filled room from burning incense and scented candles. So many refreshing smells permeated the air. The soft jazz in the background added a touch of tranquility. As they became one with the environment a man was standing on stage reading some excerpts from his book. They soon became one with him and his poetry spoke to them. *It was like they no longer existed* but were completely connected with the man on stage. He began reading a poem entitled *Words,* that read:

Words are so powerful,
Infinite fields of energy,
Expressions of thoughts,
Manifestations of what was once hidden.
They can build you up,
Then tear you down.
They can make you laugh,
Or make you cry.
Sometimes when they're not spoken,
The atmosphere is more tense,
They can mean a whole lot,
Or make no sense.
They can make you think about things you never thought of.

The poem was followed up by a thunderous applause and the man began speaking:

"Thank you, thank you. Ladies and Gentleman that was my final poem tonight and was from page 62 of my book entitled *Caressed Spirits*. This book is available for purchase tonight (he held up a copy of the book). I would like to thank all of my students for your attendance and for being smart enough to be here to receive extra credit (chuckle). I also want to thank all of you for being attentive to listen to me as I presented the story of **Baby B** and **Baby A** prior to that recitation. You see, **Baby B** and **Baby A** are really polar opposites reflecting my best and worst self and also your best and worst self. When the wrong words are *repeatedly* spoken it can have a negative impact on our development. When the right words are spoken *repeatedly* it has a positive impact. I chose to place **Baby B** before **Baby A** although A is *alphabetically before B* to show that the weaker self was going backwards. Both **Baby B** and **Baby A** are present in me and us tonight. Let's give ourselves a round of applause for coming to this point of acceptance."

The man continued:

"Like **Baby B** and **Baby A** I was born on May 25, 1972 and grew in an environment that was equally conflicted. There was an equal share of negative and positive messages so my growing environment was sometimes reflective of both **Baby B** and **Baby A**. That wasn't the case for everyone around me. Can you imagine what happens to children that don't have a balance but are the recipients of countless *curse words*? How do they end up? What kinds of victims are produced when children believe *they will never or could never be* anything of substance? **Baby B** and **Baby A** overall is a metaphor which reflects those dynamics. Inherent in the story is aspects that included friendships, relationships and various interactions as a child being confronted with *curse words*. It is also a metaphor that reflects a home environment that is responsible for murdering the spirit of children. The first blow generally begins at home.

The second blow is undoubtedly the school system. Education, unfortunately, becomes *the killing fields* for negative childhood development for some while fostering a positive self-image for others. **Baby B** and **Baby A** become two extremes of how children are encouraged or discouraged and also the blatant or subtle usage of *curse words* in a failing educational environment. Using the wrong words as motivators like *you'll never be anything of importance* with your behavior or you *can't be doctors, lawyers* or *a celebrity* if you don't change your behavior is perpetuating the *curse words* that contribute to the negative behavior in the first place. Sadly many educators don't understand this and are ill equipped to deal with the root cause of the behavioral problems.

So later in the story, we see the *choices* both **Baby B** and **Baby A** make that take their lives in different directions. As stated in the story these choices are the result of negative or positive thinking. Almost every day we are presented with something where our thinking will determine our success or failure. How many times have you said to yourself that *you can do something* or *you can master or conquer something* and saw the positive effects of that kind of thinking? On the flip side, how does doubt, disbelief, adverse thinking or our usage of *curse words* like *I can't, it's impossible, I'm not capable or any limiting, crippling word or phrase* affect the outcome? The discussion that happens between **Baby B** and **Baby A** later symbolizes our daily internal dialog that often becomes a mental, spiritual and emotional conflict. When our natural human desire to excel is confronted with self-doubt and negative feelings that result from *curse words* the outcome is seldom positive.

So **Baby B** being lost later in the story represents our state after being consumed with curse words that create self-doubt. When he was lying in a fetal position it was symbolic of going back into the womb that helped to foster his negative state of mind.

Ultimately like **Baby B** we must become vulnerable and fully expose ourselves to what we have become and finally come to grips with ourselves in order to *embrace* who we are capable of being to make our transformation. Being *fully clothed* with positive *transformational language* is the only solution that will allow us to see ourselves while on the road to recovery. We must learn to remove the curse or those *back WORDS we believed in* growing up that made us go backwards like **Baby B**. That's when we'll move forward like **Baby A**.

You all may be asking, why did I continue to refer to both of these characters as babies long after they transitioned through the various stages of human development? Research tells us that prior to conception seeds are being *planted* but the baby is significant because it represents the stage of human development where the initial seeds are being *watered*. It is that stage that I wanted us to look at and for us to see where we start going wrong.

In conclusion, it is here tonight that I will introduce the title of my new book called "***You're Daddy Wasn't Shit so You're not Going to be Shit: Removing the Harmful Effects of Curse Words***". Hopefully, after reading what is presented we will all become better parents, teachers, community, and world. My desire is for us to become fully aware of the power of the words we use and how using the wrong words can place limitations on those that are under our care, supervision and guidance. Thank you all for listening to me and I hope that what I said was taken in the right spirit and will bear fruit. I want to leave you all with this final poem:

To these parents and educators

I'm highly disappointed

So I've been anointed

With the pen

Wrote my feelings in a book

To look at where the shallow shit begins

She said, He said, They said

Your daddy wasn't shit

So you're not going to be shit

Those words hit

Like domestic violence

Silence the spirit of innocence

Rang loud like sirens

I sense

Curse words

Hurtful words

Disperse those words

Devastating

Steadily stagnating

Target

Aim

Struck

Now when little Johnny run amuck

You call him a little dumb fuck

When you're the fucker

That was fuckin who

Fucked you

And left you for a more pleasing cum

FUCK

Nah fuck the bullshit

He should've pulled quick

But he released like words

And pulled shit

To kill the peace
Increase the bullshit
Took too many miles fuck an inch
That's bullshit
Compared to his stench
Bullshit actually smells like roses
Rose's abortion would've been heaven
To the twins Evelyn and Evan
Kevin left when they were seven
Having too many domestic disputes
Not cute
Words now used to verbally abuse
Your daddy wasn't shit
So you're not going to be shit
Words hit
Shit
Bitch
Fuck
Shit
I'm
Stuck
Creating negative attitudes
Now claiming
Nothing in the context
Is too complex
Your content is constantly
Containing condescending

Consistent complaining

Convinced you're

Consistently gaining

But your children are convicted

By your corrupt communication

Careless conversation and lack of conscious

Leaving them consumed with curses

Lack of confidence, courage

But remaining

With curse words

Never teaching them that genius is common

When a penis is common

Impregnating ladies, birthing babies

Generational curses, no rehearses

All learning the same script

Your daddy wasn't shit

So you're not going to be shit

So check the subject

Because this isn't it

Re-read the book.

The *After* Thought

Today it would be hard for us to conceive of a world where people were actually thinking, speaking and reproducing other human beings at a higher frequency. Our minds *can't* fathom the kind of world where children knew their divine human potential before becoming adults. Believe it or not, that kind of world existed.

A world existed where man viewed himself in line with the divine and didn't make a separation from himself and GOD. Children were reared to manifest their higher selves and were never taught *any limitations* so the thought of *impossibility* was nonexistent. Everyone vibrated on a higher frequency but at some point that all changed. In the religious contexts that change symbolizes the fall of man.

In the kind of world we live in today, "*being the shit*" is actually a compliment and is the highest plateau some aspire to. On the flip side "*not being shit*" makes many feel devalued when in essence the reference that is upheld is also demeaning. This book brings light to those real curse words. This does not suggest that using profane words to children is not a problem, it is. The focus of this book, however, is to look at the words we take for granted that I believe are more harmful. These words are the negative words that often form our beliefs.

Deepak Chopra wrote in an article called your beliefs can change your life that:

"The most powerful beliefs are the ones I call core beliefs, because they tell you who you are. If someone deeply believes "I'm a winner" and someone else believes "I am unlovable," the outcome of their core

beliefs will be very different. It's critical to hold positive core beliefs and to activate them in your daily life. The more you activate your core beliefs, the more dynamic and transformed your reality will be."

When I was about 16 years of age I was introduced to the wisdom of three wise men that constantly taught the importance of transformational language in their teachings and made me look and reflect on my *core beliefs*. The first wise man taught the second wise man who taught the third wise man. The second wise man instructed that, *"You cannot change a person's condition until you change their thinking."* Understanding that everything came after thought these words made perfect sense to me. He would then provide information that would go to the root of his student's negative thinking and tell them how powerful they were and how they can accomplish anything because there is no such thing as *impossibility*. The third student profoundly would tell his students that *"He who gives you the diameter of your knowledge prescribes the circumference of your activity"*. His methodology was to attack his students negative core beliefs that were the result of things taught to them by their parents, teachers and society at large and provide them with a more powerful and positive view of themselves.

This kind of instruction reared students that felt they were capable of excelling at any and everything. It also gave them *knowledge of self* which refuted any contradictory message or *curse words* that would make them feel limited in their abilities. What I found most fascinating about what they were teaching was the notion that *Man is God and God is Man*. Ascribing divine qualities to human beings held us to a higher standard. It also gave us a greater connection to the creator (so above) because we understood that the divine power was within us (so below) making us capable of anything we put our minds to. That kind of instruction was paramount because it eliminated the negative thinking and despair.

When society fosters negative thinking and despair there becomes an inordinate need for relief and intervention. What I found interesting while pondering on where this book would fall is the capitalization of human despair that converts into the third largest grossing genre in literature. That is Religious/Inspirational which brings in $720 Million in revenue annually. That is also why I referenced those that fall into this genre throughout this book. The only two other genre's leading were Romance/Erotica at $1.44 Billion followed by Crime/Mystery at $728.2 Million.

If human beings are taught correctly and the appropriate language is used to foster healthy views of self, there would be no need for books like this; religious and inspirational literature would lack an audience and all motivational speakers would cease to exist. Unfortunately, that is not the case and there hasn't been a major shift in language to create more positive behavior, it is actually getting worse. This is where you and I come in. We have to be the change agents that make and promote better word choices. Instead of saying *I'm sorry* simply apologize, instead of saying *you can't do something* simply work on a way to get it done. Instead of saying what *you're not capable of*, think about how capable you really are and how nothing limits you but yourself. Try some "Psycho-Cybernetics" that states it takes *21 days to make or break a habit* (smile) and do it.

Just imagine, if there isn't a shift in language starting with you and I serving as educators to parents we will sentence another generation to *curse words. This will continue the cycle of* creating more children that enter into schools with teachers that aren't adequately equipped because many of them were victims themselves. These children would then become adults that enter into dysfunctional relationships and apply for jobs with supervisors or managers that also perpetuate the same curse words as a form of motivation for employees. On the flip side if this transformational language becomes the *afterthought* after negative thought we have accomplished our goal.

In conclusion, wouldn't you like to live in a world where people are actually thinking, speaking and reproducing other human beings at a higher frequency? Wouldn't you like to live in the kind of world where children know their divine human potential before becoming adults? A world can exist again where man views himself in line with the divine and doesn't make a separation from himself and GOD. Children can be reared to manifest their higher selves and never ever receive teachings that foster *limitations*. In this kind of world, the thought of *impossibility* will become nonexistent. Removing the harmful effects of curse words can create that kind of world but that world first has to start in you. Change your language and change your world.

Acknowledgements

First and foremost I would like to thank God for the gift of writing and for his divine intervention in our affairs. I would also like to thank him for the Exalted Christ and his Grace and Reminder for depositing their spirit in me. I would like to thank my mother Grace Glover and father David Glover for the gift of life. I am extremely grateful to my wisdom and understanding Krystle Patrick and Sanaa Fatirah Muhammad. You two have motivated me tremendously. I love you both.

I would like to thank my brothers David Glover the Controversial Counselor and D and G Enterprises and also my younger brother, business partner and right hand man Dedrick Muhammad for both of your contribution to this project. We still have so much more work ahead of us. I would like to thank my biggest supporter, business partner and brother in faith and spirit Keith Muhammad for being the real mouth and muscle for Luv4self Enterprises. I would like to thank my one and only sister Natasha Glover. I want to thank a great friend and former colleague of mine, Nicole Webb, for our discussion on creating a small book that was designed to make a large impact. Thank you.

I would like to acknowledge my entire family (too many to name) and also the Petersons and Patrick's of Baltimore MD and Trinidad and Tobago. I want to thank Luv4self Enterprises, Luv4self Publishing, Beverly Black Johnson and Bruce George and the entire Gumbo for the Soul International family, Tribe Family Channel, Genius is Common and the 5th Element of Hip Hop Symposium. I would like to thank Theo Edwards and Travis Case of Mason Diction Entertainment for the video promotional piece. I would like to thank Dr. Alicia Harvey Smith for all of her motivation and support. I would be remiss if I didn't mention all of my friends that grew up with me on North Avenue and Unity Park in Niagara Falls, New York. My East Ferry to Walden and Genesee family in Buffalo, New York, My Buffalo State College family, friends and colleagues at The Community College of Baltimore County and Baltimore City Community College, Johns Hopkins University and the entire Diplomas Now/Talent Development Secondary Program for the marvelous work done in education. I would like to thank all of the Holcombe L. Rucker High school Staff in the Bronx, New York and everyone else that crossed paths with me and impacted me in some way in producing this project. Last but not least all of those that contributed to the Luv4self Go Fund Me campaign. You all are so appreciated. The drive continues as my drive continues. To all of those I failed to mention, charge it to my head and not my heart. I love all of you for your continued prayers, encouragement and support. I hope you have enjoyed this book.

Carlos Muhammad is an Author, Poet, Speaker and Educator. He spends his time between Baltimore, Md and New York City as a School Transformation Facilitator/Community School Director for Johns Hopkins University. Carlos Muhammad is presently working on the release of his second long awaited volume of poetry entitled "Penspiration: The Dual Nature of the Pen", the follow up to Caressed Spirits: Poetic Thoughts and Reflections from a Black Man's Perspective and other publications. Carlos travels presenting poetry, seminars, workshops and forums for the purpose of educating and enlightening.

www.ingramcontent.com/pod-product-compliance
Lightning Source LLC
Chambersburg PA
CBHW072039060426
42449CB00010BA/2356